Flowchart Smart

POLLUTION

Richard and Louise Spilsbury

Gareth Stevens Publishing

Please visit our website, **www.garethstevens.com**.
For a free color catalog of all our high-quality books,
call toll free 1-800-542-2595 or fax 1-877-542-2596.

Cataloging-in-Publication Data
Names: Spilsbury, Richard. | Spilsbury, Louise.
Title: Pollution / Richard and Louise Spilsbury.
Description: New York : Gareth Stevens Publishing, 2019. | Series: Flowchart smart | Includes glossary and index.
Identifiers: ISBN 9781538234914 (pbk.) | ISBN 9781538234921 (library bound)
Subjects: LCSH: Pollution--Juvenile literature. | Refuse and refuse disposal--Juvenile literature.
Classification: LCC TD176.S677 2019 | DDC 363.73--dc23

First Edition

Published in 2019 by
Gareth Stevens Publishing
111 East 14th Street, Suite 349
New York, NY 10003

Produced for Gareth Stevens by Calcium
Editors: Sarah Eason and Harriet McGregor
Designer: Emma DeBanks
Picture researcher: Rachel Blount

Picture credits: Cover: Shutterstock: Denk Creative; Inside: Shutterstock: A3pfamily: p. 41t; Mohamed Abdulraheem: p. 27b; Anticiclo: p. 14; Anton Ivanov: pp. 34–35; Eganova Antonina: p. 31tc; Arnain: p. 5t; Gavin Baker Photography: p. 19t; Brown32: p. 23; Volodymyr Burdiak: pp. 40–41; Danylyukk1: p. 17; Denk Creative: pp. 11b, 34b, 35c; Dragon Images: pp. 44–45; Fenkieandreas: p. 37t; Fireofheart: p. 39; Graphbottles: p. 35t; Hurst Photo: p. 45t; Nina Janesikova: pp. 4–5; Jelloyd: p. 31t; JonahWong: p. 9; M2020: pp. 6–7; Nikiteev Konstantin: p. 6t; Maureen Perez: pp. 1, 13b; Peteri: p. 21r; Photoiconix: p. 43; Panotthorn Phuhual: p. 33; Dewi Putra: pp. 20–21; Rasulov: p. 11t; Robuart: p. 29b; Salajean: pp. 28–29; Steinar: pp. 4bl, 7b, 10t; StevenK: pp. 26–27; Stockphoto-graf: pp. 24–25; Zick Svift: pp. 36–37; Testing: pp. 10–11; Abramov Timur: p. 25t; Ben Trahair: pp. 18–19; Vandathai: p. 15; Vectors Bang: pp. 4tr, 18tr, 18bl; Visual Generation: p. 15l; Whitelook: pp. 12–13; Mark Winfrey: pp. 30–31; Wk1003mike: p. 6b; Wongimam: p. 29t.

Printed in the United States of America

CPSIA compliance information: Batch #CW19GS: For further information contact Gareth Stevens, New York, New York at 1-800-542-2595.

Contents

Chapter 1

What Is Pollution?

Litter on the street, smoke in the air, and sewage flowing into waterways are all forms of pollution. Pollution is when any part of the **environment** around us is made dirty and unusable.

Some pollution has natural causes. When a volcano erupts it ejects poisonous gases and clouds of ash into the air. When these **pollutants** fall as rain, they enter rivers, soak into the soil, and can kill plants and animals. However, most of the pollution in the world is caused by human activities. Factories dump waste into rivers, people drop trash in the streets, and oil leaks from trucks and cars.

Mount Agung in Bali, Indonesia, spews volcanic ash, a natural source of pollution, into the air.

Many of the world's beaches are polluted with trash and domestic waste.

Pollution builds up and gradually becomes an environmental problem over a long period of time. For example, the trash that enters the world's oceans builds up piece by piece, a plastic bag here and an old fishing line there. This kind of waste breaks down very slowly, so over time, the waste in the oceans creates a major problem. Other pollution happens much more quickly. When a ship carrying oil across the ocean accidentally spills its contents, it instantly pollutes the water all around it.

Get Smart!

In 2011, a giant tsunami wave, caused by an earthquake off the coast of Japan, washed about 22 million tons (20 million t) of debris out into the ocean. The waste included plastics, motorcycles, boats, and other items. Some sank and some washed up on distant coastlines.

The Impact of Pollution

An **ecosystem** is a community of living things and the place in which they live. A lake and the plants, fish, and other animals that live there is an ecosystem. When an ecosystem is polluted, the natural balance is disturbed. The pollution affects the living things and their homes in different ways.

Each of the different **organisms** in an ecosystem forms a link in a **food chain**. Plants are eaten by animals, and these animals are themselves food for other animals. The living things in a lake ecosystem rely on its water, the air above it, and the mud on the lake floor. These elements provide places to live, oxygen to breathe, and **nutrients** to grow.

Imagine that a truck dumped **toxic** waste into a wetland. Frogs and other amphibians have a very thin skin, through which they can absorb oxygen. If they absorb toxic materials in this way, the poisons build up in their bodies. If the amphibians in the wetland die, the birds that feed on them and the fish that feed on tadpoles (frogs' offspring) go hungry. This means that there are fewer fish for humans and other animals to eat. Without frogs to eat the mosquitoes that live around the wetland, the mosquito populations grow. Anyone living nearby will be at a greater risk of catching diseases passed on by mosquitoes.

Water pollution poisons and sometimes kills wildlife such as fish.

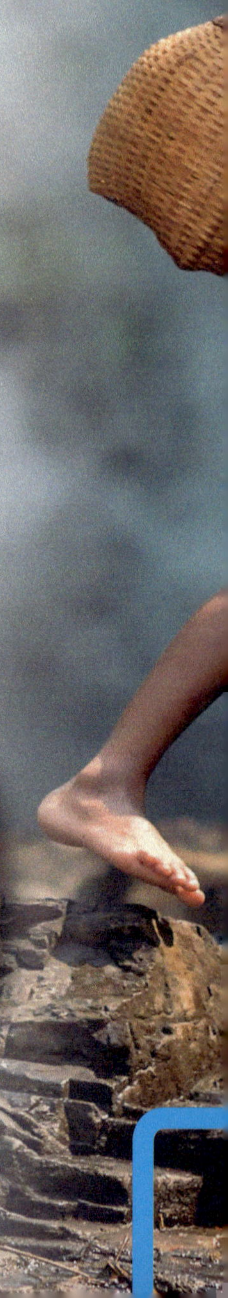

Catching and eating fish that contain pollutants can damage the human body.

Get Smart!

Recent studies have found that polluted air, water, and soils kill at least 9 million people around the world every year. That is one out of every six deaths that occur around the world. The majority of the deaths caused by pollution occur in poorer countries.

Get flowchart smart!

Passing on Pollution

Follow the steps in this flowchart to see how one type of pollution affects many other living things, including people.

A truck dumps toxic waste into a wetland.

Without frogs to eat mosquitoes, mosquito populations grow. Mosquitoes bite people and may pass on any diseases they carry.

There are fewer fish to eat.

Flowchart Smart

Frogs absorb toxic materials through their skin. These toxins build up in their bodies.

Some of the frogs die.

The birds that feed on the frogs and the fish that feed on the tadpoles (frogs' offspring) do not have enough food, and some die.

Chapter 2
Air Pollution

Earth is surrounded by layers of gases, which form the **atmosphere**. These gases include oxygen, which humans and other animals need to breathe and live. The atmosphere is polluted when dust **particles**, fumes, smoke, and other gases are added to it.

The most common source of air pollution comes from the burning of **fossil fuels**. Cars, trucks, trains, ships, and airplanes all burn fossil fuels to power their engines and make them move. This releases extremely small particles of dust and soot, and invisible gases such as carbon monoxide and nitrogen dioxide.

In big cities such as Beijing in China, people wear face masks so that they do not inhale the air pollution.

Get Smart!

According to the American Lung Association (ALA), nearly half of all Americans live in areas with unhealthy levels of air pollution.

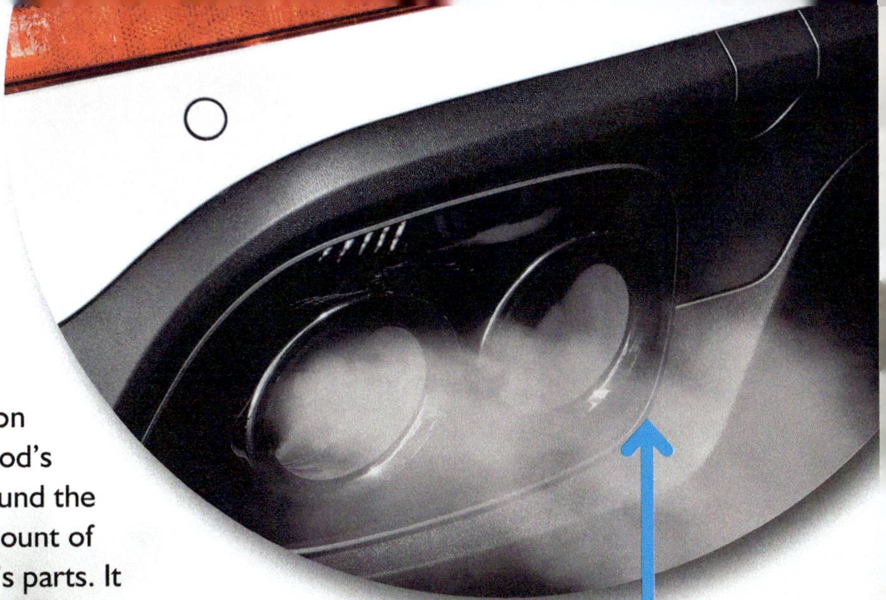

The pollution from vehicles causes serious health problems. Extra nitrogen dioxide in the atmosphere inflames the lining in the lungs and increases the risk of lung diseases and other breathing problems. Carbon monoxide reduces the blood's ability to carry oxygen around the body. This reduces the amount of oxygen reaching the body's parts. It causes chest pains and worsens heart disease. Badly polluted air can cause heart or lung disease and early death.

Transportation is one of the largest causes of air pollution in the United States.

Power and Pollution

A power plant is a kind of factory that produces electricity. In most power plants, electricity is made using either coal or natural gas as fuel. These fuels are burned to heat water. Steam from the water turns the blades of a propeller-like machine called a turbine. The turbine spins another machine called a generator, which generates the electricity.

Coal formed from plants that died millions of years ago. It contains lignin, a plant material that contains a lot of carbon. Fuels need oxygen to burn. The **combustion**, or burning, reaction that takes place releases **energy**. When coal burns, its carbon combines with oxygen from the air to make new particles of **carbon dioxide**.

Pollution from coal-fired power plants leads to smog that can drift over entire cities.

Along with other gases, such as methane and **water vapor**, carbon dioxide is a **greenhouse gas**. Carbon dioxide rises into the atmosphere. Once there, it absorbs heat energy and keeps heat from escaping from Earth into space. It acts a little like the glass in a greenhouse. The more carbon dioxide there is in the atmosphere, the more heat energy is absorbed and the hotter Earth becomes. This effect is known as **global warming**.

Get Smart!

Burning fossil fuels also releases nitrogen, which can combine with oxygen to form nitrogen oxides. Nitrogen oxides are greenhouse gases. They react with substances in the air to form smog. Smog reduces visibility, damages plants, and increases the risk of conditions such as asthma and lung damage.

Electricity production in power plants generates the largest share of greenhouse gas emissions.

Acid Rain

Acid rain is a type of rainfall that has been made acidic by pollution. The gases emitted when fossil fuels are burned can create acid rain. Acid rain damages crops, forests, and materials such as stonework on buildings, and can harm animals and other plants.

When coal and oil are burned, sulfur dioxide and nitrogen oxides enter the atmosphere. These gases combine with oxygen, water, and other chemicals to form sulfuric and nitric acids. These acids are present in droplets of water in the air. More and more droplets of acidic water are blown around by the wind and gather together in clouds. Eventually they fall as acid rain, snow, or hail.

Acid rain harms trees by limiting the nutrients available to them or by releasing poisonous substances from the soil.

Acid rain weakens the structure of some types of stone and damages it.

When acid rain soaks into the ground, it leaches, or takes away, nutrients and **minerals** from the soil, which trees and other plants need to grow properly. At the same time, acid rain causes aluminum to be released from the soil. Aluminum is a substance that makes it difficult for tree roots to absorb water from the soil. Aluminum released from the soil can also end up in lakes and streams. Along with acid rain, this changes the water in the lakes and streams and harms fish and other wildlife.

Get Smart!

Acid rain can damage statues and buildings made of limestone. Sulfuric acid in rainwater reacts with calcium carbonate in the limestone and erodes it.

Get flowchart smart!

Acid Rain in Action

Follow the flowchart for a closer look at how acid rain is formed.

Fossil fuels are burned in vehicle engines, power plants, and factories.

Gradually, more and more droplets of acidic water gather in clouds.

Eventually they reach Earth as rain, snow, and hail. Collectively, these are known as acid rain.

Flowchart Smart

Pollutant gases such as sulfur dioxide and nitrogen oxides are produced.

These gases rise up in the atmosphere. They combine with oxygen, water, and other chemicals, and form sulfuric and nitric acids.

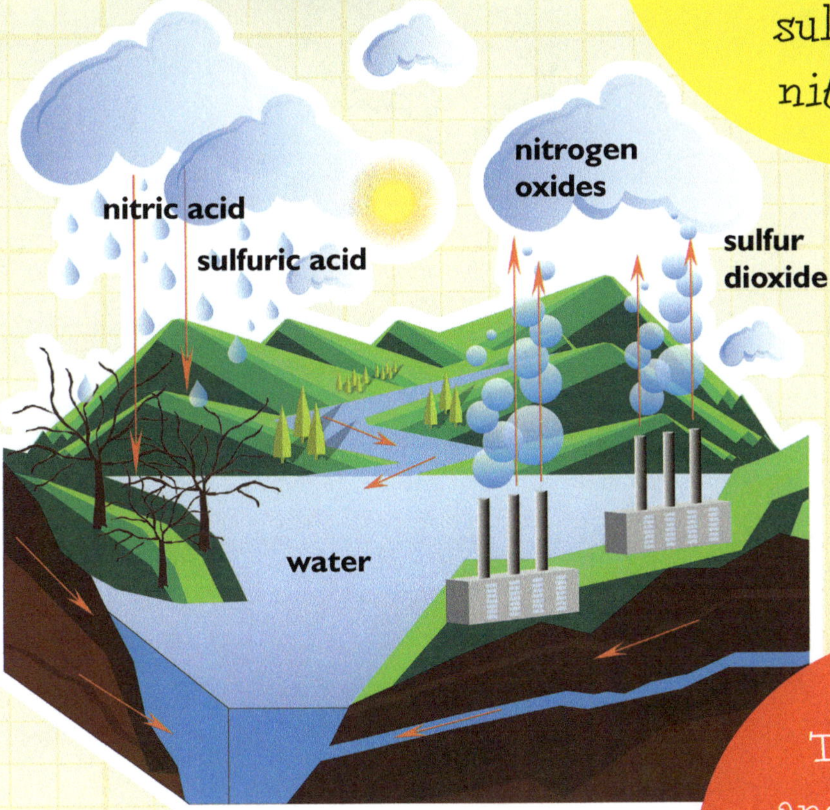

The sulfuric and nitric acids are present in droplets of water in the air.

Chapter 3

Land Pollution

Land pollution is caused by a variety of activities. Soils are damaged by mining, waste disposal, accidental spills, illegal dumping, and the use of chemical sprays on farms. Trash dropped on streets or left behind by hikers in wild places are also forms of land pollution.

Farming is a leading source of pollution in some countries. **Pesticides** are chemicals used by farmers to kill insects that eat plant crops. When farmers spray pesticides onto fields, for example from airplanes, these chemicals also pollute land around the fields. Additionally, many pesticides do not just kill the target pest. They can also poison or kill other insects in and around the fields, many of which are vital to Earth's ecosystems, such as bees.

Chemicals help farmers grow crops, such as this cotton, for increasing populations.

Pesticides also kill soil **microorganisms**. These are very tiny living things found in soil, such as **bacteria**. They are often known as decomposers, because they help decompose, or break down, **organic** matter such as leaves into nutrients that plants use to grow. If too many chemicals are used on an area of soil, reducing the numbers of microorganisms in it, the soil becomes less fertile. That means fewer plants and crops can thrive there.

Research has shown that up to 95 percent of pesticides applied in this way miss their target. Instead they land on neighboring land, waterways, homes, and yards.

Get Smart!

Many of the farmers who grow cotton plants use very large amounts of pesticides. While only 2.5 percent of the world's cropland is used for growing cotton, cotton farmers use more than 20 percent of the world's pesticides.

Waste and Landfills

As the world's population increases, the amount of waste we create increases, too. Much of this waste ends up in landfills. These are places where garbage is buried in the ground. Even when waste is disposed of correctly like this, it can still cause pollution.

Some types of waste are biodegradable. This means that they naturally rot away in the soil without doing any harm. When microorganisms in surface soil layers break down organic waste, such as food, they can return the nutrients to the soil, which helps new plants grow. Microorganisms that break down waste deep within a landfill do so without oxygen. The waste products from their activity include carbon dioxide and methane gas. Methane is up to 30 times more damaging than other greenhouse gases.

In some places, cows produce toxic milk because they eat garbage.

Some of the waste piled in landfill sites is toxic. Metals and other chemical wastes can leak from batteries and **contaminate** the environment when they break down. Organic waste creates leachate, the liquid that leaches from a landfill. When rain falls on the garbage in the landfill, it gradually seeps through to the lower layers. The rainwater collects chemicals from the rotting waste. These chemicals can react together to create new and even more dangerous waste. For example, building waste such as gypsum plaster reacts with leachate and forms hazardous hydrogen sulfide gas. These pollutants flow with the leachate into surrounding soil and waterways.

This landfill site has made a nearby lake toxic, filling it with dangerous chemicals.

Get Smart!

Many new landfill sites have leachate collection systems to keep it from polluting the surrounding land and water. Some try to capture the methane gas that escapes from landfills and use it to produce energy.

Get flowchart smart!

Landfills and Leachate

Follow the steps in this flowchart to learn how leachate forms at landfills.

Garbage disposal trucks bring waste collected from cities and dump it into large holes in the ground called landfill sites.

The chemicals react with other chemicals to create new ones.

These pollutants flow in the liquid leachate into the surrounding soil.

Flowchart Smart

Toxic chemicals and metals leak from batteries and other materials when they break down.

When rain falls on the garbage in the landfill it gradually seeps through to lower layers.

As rainwater moves through the waste it collects chemicals.

Chapter 4

Water Pollution

Water pollution is caused when people accidentally or purposely release harmful substances into rivers, lakes, seas, and oceans. Leachate from landfills is one form of water pollution, but there are many others. Polluted waterways harm wildlife living in them, but they are bad for humans, too. When pollutants seep down to **groundwater** sources, they end up in our homes when we turn on our faucets.

Sewage is the largest and most common source of water pollution. Sewage pipes carry flushed waste away from our sinks and bathrooms. In some parts of the world, this sewage is pumped directly into rivers, lakes, and other waterways without being treated. Even when sewer systems take sewage to treatment plants, millions of gallons of sewage escapes from leaky pipes and old treatment plants, and enters waterways.

Urban runoff is rainwater that flows over surfaces such as driveways and streets. This water often collects in gutters and pipes, and flows into sewage systems. As the water crosses these urban surfaces, it picks up pollutants. If this water is not treated and is released into rivers and oceans, it can cause a threat to both human health and the environment. Many water animals cannot survive in polluted water. Untreated human sewage contains bacteria that can cause disease.

This sewage pipe is pumping human waste directly onto a coral reef.

Drains like these carry urban runoff down into sewage pipes. Today, there is more urban runoff because there are fewer areas of land into which water can soak.

Get Smart!

Pollution can affect the water we use for leisure, too. Scientists believe as many as 3.5 million Americans get sick each year after swimming, boating, fishing, or otherwise touching water they thought was safe.

Oceans Under Attack

Ocean pollution is a major world problem. Some of the waste and chemicals that are washed down sewage pipes flow directly into oceans, but one of the worst forms of ocean pollution is plastic.

Most marine pollution is solid waste such as old fishing nets and plastic bags. Plastic floats and takes hundreds of years to rot. These pieces of plastic harm ocean animals that mistake them for food. Ocean animals also eat tiny pieces of plastic called microplastics. Humans consume these when they eat contaminated seafood. Other animals are injured or killed by waste because they become entangled in it. Animals trapped in fishing nets cannot swim to find food and they may starve to death.

This beach in Mumbai, India, is covered with tons of garbage that have washed ashore.

Ocean liners and other ships may dump sewage and other waste directly into the ocean. Tankers are large ocean-going ships that transport oil from oil rigs at sea. If oil rigs or tankers spill oil into the water, it causes a lot of damage. Oil pollution clogs fur and feathers, preventing animals and birds from keeping warm and waterproof.

Another problem is ocean acidification. Ocean waters absorb massive amounts of the carbon dioxide released by burning fossil fuels. When carbon dioxide **dissolves** in seawater, carbonic acid forms. Carbonic acid prevents the shells of shellfish from developing properly and it is also suspected of preventing some fish from being able to have young.

Get Smart!

The Great Pacific Garbage Patch is an enormous floating area of trash that is about twice the size of Texas. It stretches halfway between Hawaii and California in the Pacific Ocean. The vast expanse of waste is held in place by swirling underwater currents.

Hundreds of thousands of sea turtles and other marine creatures are killed by pollution each year.

Effects of Mining

Mining is an important industry in which minerals are removed from the ground. Mining provides us with fossil fuels for energy, stone for building, and metals to make a huge range of objects, from soda cans to airplanes. However, mining also causes pollution.

Some of the world's larger mines use bulldozers and diggers to extract metals and minerals from under the ground. When miners dig into the earth, minerals from deep below the surface are brought upward. Here, they can react with oxygen and create pollutants. For example, when iron salts and sulfur-containing materials react with oxygen they dissolve in water and make it highly acidic.

This area of Romania was polluted by waste from a local copper mine.

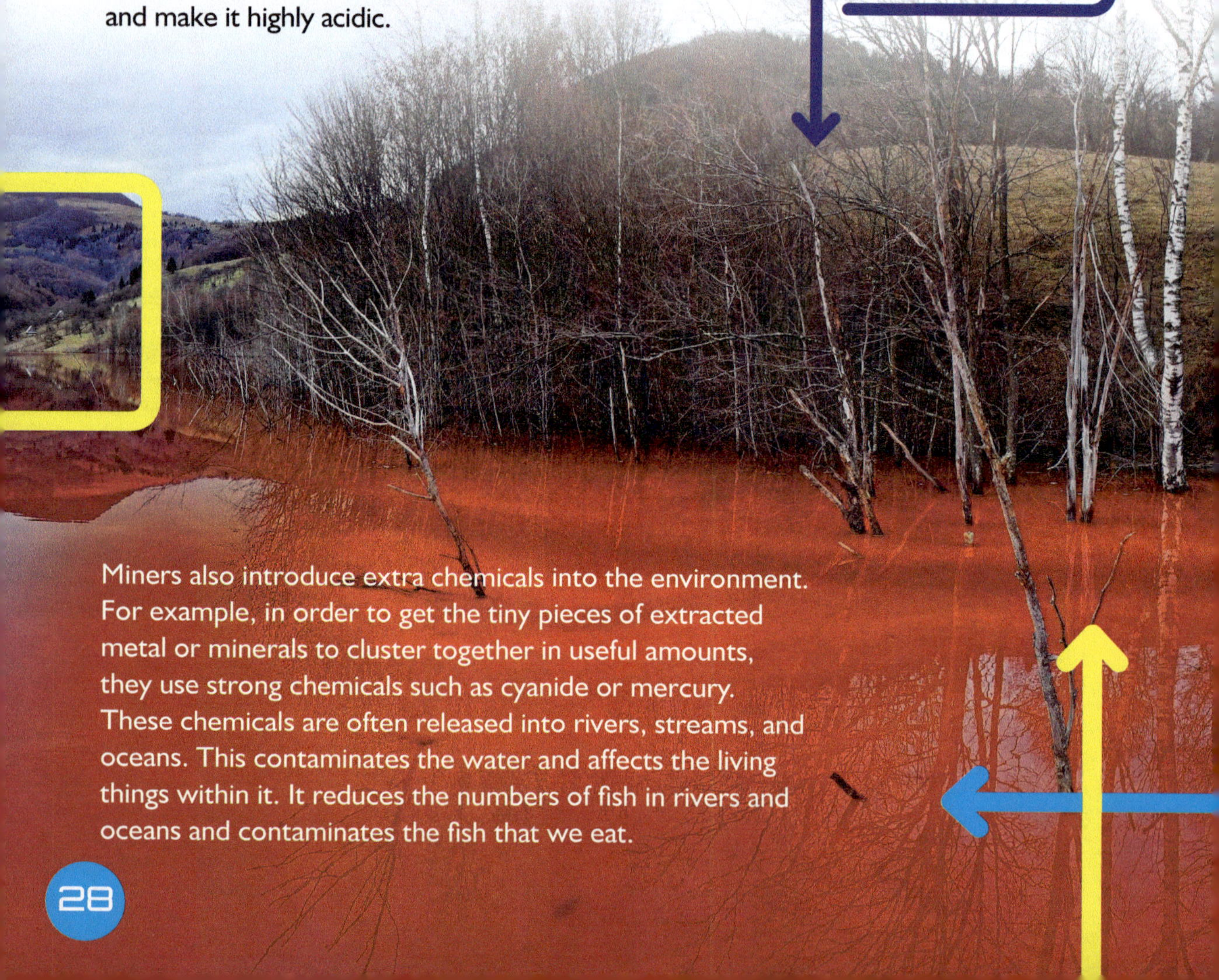

Miners also introduce extra chemicals into the environment. For example, in order to get the tiny pieces of extracted metal or minerals to cluster together in useful amounts, they use strong chemicals such as cyanide or mercury. These chemicals are often released into rivers, streams, and oceans. This contaminates the water and affects the living things within it. It reduces the numbers of fish in rivers and oceans and contaminates the fish that we eat.

Open pit mines also destroy the natural environment, leaving insects, birds, and other animals with nowhere to live.

Get Smart!

Mercury is highly toxic and can cause serious illness and death in humans and animals, but it is still used to extract gold from mines in developing countries. The United Nations estimates that mining exposes up to 15 million workers in 70 different countries to mercury poisoning.

Industrial Runoff

Industries, from farms to factories, are major sources of water pollution. Water is used in factories to make products, to cool down factory machines, and at high pressure to clean and cut metals. When factories discharge the used water it often contains pollutants and it is sometimes released directly into waterways. Many industrial plants use fresh water to carry away waste from the plant and into rivers, lakes, and oceans.

When farmers apply pesticides and chemicals to soils, some are washed deep into the ground by rainwater. The pollutants can seep into underground water sources. When people dig wells and bore holes to get water from these sources, it must be checked for pollution and cleaned before it can be used.

Fertilizers contain nitrates and phosphates that help crops grow bigger and better. When rain falls on farmers' fields, it can wash fertilizer from the soil into nearby rivers and lakes. When nitrates and phosphates build up in the water, **algae** use the extra nutrients to grow. The nutrients can cause a dramatic increase in algae at a pond's surface. This is called an algal bloom. The bloom keeps sunlight from reaching other water plants, which then die. Bacteria break down the dead plants and use up the oxygen in the water, leaving too little for fish and other aquatic life to survive. This process is called eutrophication.

Some industries discharge untreated wastewater directly into the environment.

An algal bloom can grow and cover an entire pond.

Get Smart!

Agriculture covers nearly one-half of the land in the United States. This creates widespread opportunities for nutrients that originate on fields to run off into streams and groundwater.

Get flowchart smart!

How Eutrophication Works

Follow the steps in this flowchart to discover how algal blooms harm freshwater wildlife.

Farmers spray fertilizers containing nutrients called nitrates and phosphates on crops to help them grow bigger and better.

The algal bloom keeps sunlight from reaching other water plants, which then die.

Bacteria break down the dead plants and use up the oxygen in the water, leaving too little for fish and other aquatic life to survive. This whole process is called eutrophication.

Rain washes fertilizers into nearby bodies of water.

Nitrates and phosphates build up in the water and algae use the extra nutrients to grow.

The nutrients cause a dramatic increase in algae on the water surface. This is called an algal bloom.

Flowchart Smart

Chapter 5

Pollution Problems

Pollution impacts plants, animals, and the ecosystems to which they belong. It puts human health at risk, reduces the amount of food and fresh clean water available to us, and spoils the beauty of the natural environment.

The health problems caused by pollution vary around the world. Cities where there is slow, heavy traffic suffer the worst air pollution. People who work with polluting chemicals are also under threat. As many as 25 million farm workers worldwide experience unintentional pesticide poisoning each year.

In some parts of developing countries, where people lack **sanitation systems** and have a limited supply of fresh clean water, many people suffer from diarrhea. It is thought that around 1.8 million people, mostly children, are killed by diarrhea every year. Diarrhea is caused by bacteria in dirty water. When toilet waste is flushed into rivers, it pollutes the water. People may drink the water or use it to wash in or cook with. The people consume fecal bacteria and become sick themselves with diarrhea. The bacteria are spread further if hands are not washed after going to the bathroom. More people get sick and the cycle continues.

Drinking contaminated water can transmit diseases including cholera, dysentery, typhoid, and polio.

Around 92 percent of the world's population live in a place where air pollution exceeds safe limits.

Get Smart!

Worldwide it is estimated that 2 million people, more than half of whom are in developing countries, die every year from air pollution.

Global Warming

Pollution is a global problem. One of the most damaging and life-threatening effects of pollution is global warming.

Polluting greenhouse gases, such as carbon dioxide, trap heat in Earth's atmosphere and cause global warming. The effects of global warming will cause **climate change**, a profound change in the planet's weather patterns. Some areas, such as southwest America, will have more and longer periods of drought and heat waves, when the weather is extremely hot and dry. In other parts, hurricanes and other storms will become more intense, leading to more floods. As temperatures increase, ice at the poles will melt and cause sea levels to rise, submerging low-lying islands and coastal areas.

As well as causing ocean acidification, global warming also harms oceanic food chains. Global warming increases ocean temperatures, reducing the numbers of tiny creatures called krill, which need very cold water to reproduce. Krill are food for fish, seals, whales, and other marine animals. Global warming also kills animals called polyps that make coral reefs. Coral polyps share food with the algae that live among them, but when very warm water washes over the reefs, the corals shed the algae that nourish them. The corals starve to death. Coral reefs provide many fish and other animals with food and shelter, and they protect coastlines by absorbing up to 97 percent of a wave's energy before it hits the shore.

Severe drought dries up land and makes it useless for growing crops that could feed animals and people.

When coral dies it turns white and is then described as bleached.

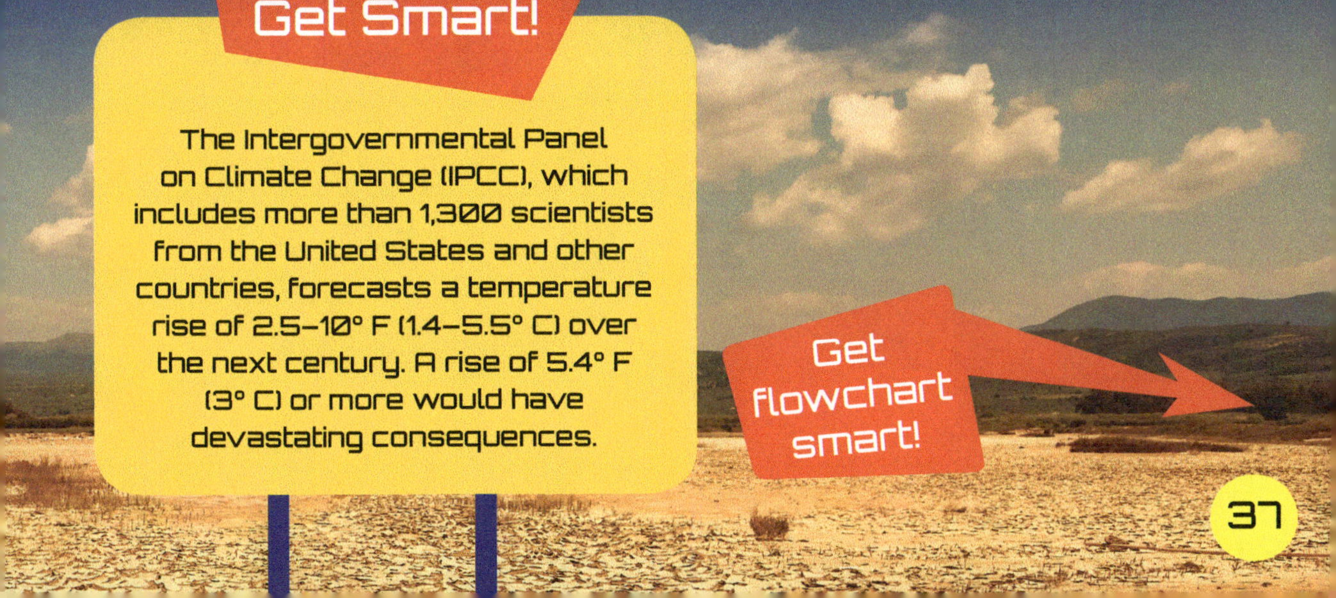

Get Smart!

The Intergovernmental Panel on Climate Change (IPCC), which includes more than 1,300 scientists from the United States and other countries, forecasts a temperature rise of 2.5–10° F (1.4–5.5° C) over the next century. A rise of 5.4° F (3° C) or more would have devastating consequences.

Get flowchart smart!

How Polluted Water Spreads Disease

Follow the steps in this flowchart to understand the dirty water disease cycle.

Toilet waste containing bacteria is flushed into rivers where it pollutes the water.

People drink the polluted water or use it for washing or cooking.

As more bacteria-filled feces are flushed into rivers and other water supplies, the disease spreads to more and more people.

Flowchart Smart

Bacteria enter the human body where they cause disease, often resulting in diarrhea.

When the sick people do not have enough water to wash their hands properly, traces of feces and bacteria on their fingers are spread to other people.

Chapter 6

Solving Pollution Problems

All over the world, scientists, governments, and others are working on ways to solve the problems of pollution. Some ideas are fairly simple, such as planting more trees. Others require bigger, more expensive changes and technology, such as renewable energy plants.

Renewable energy is electricity made from wind, moving water, or sunlight. Renewable energy will not run out, unlike fossil fuels. The major advantage of renewable forms of energy is that they do not release polluting gases. Renewable energy systems trap the movement of energy in wind and moving water, or the energy in sunlight, and convert it into electricity. If we can increase the number of renewable energy plants across the world, we can reduce the amount of greenhouse gases pumped into the atmosphere.

Wind farms are often built in high places where wind speeds are usually fast. They generate electricity.

Planting more trees is a simple way of reducing air pollution because plants remove carbon dioxide from the air. Animals breathe out carbon dioxide. Burning fossil fuels also releases carbon dioxide. Plants absorb carbon dioxide from the air and use it to make food in the process of **photosynthesis**. The carbon is stored in the plant. Animals feed on the plants, and pass the carbon along the food chain. When animals and plants die and decompose, the carbon in their bodies is returned to the atmosphere as carbon dioxide. This carbon cycle repeats again and again.

Trees also improve air quality by taking in tiny particles that would otherwise cause lung disease in those living nearby.

Get Smart!

Younger trees absorb carbon dioxide quickly while they are growing. On average, 1 acre (4,050 sq m) of new trees can store about 2.5 tons (2.3 t) of carbon in one year.

Get flowchart smart!

How the Carbon Cycle Works

This flowchart takes you through the stages in the carbon cycle.

Carbon enters the air when animals breathe out and when fossil fuels are burned.

Plants absorb carbon dioxide from the air and use it to make food in the process of photosynthesis. They store carbon in their bodies.

This carbon cycle repeats over and over. As human activities put more carbon dioxide into the air, we must plant more trees to absorb it and keep the system in balance.

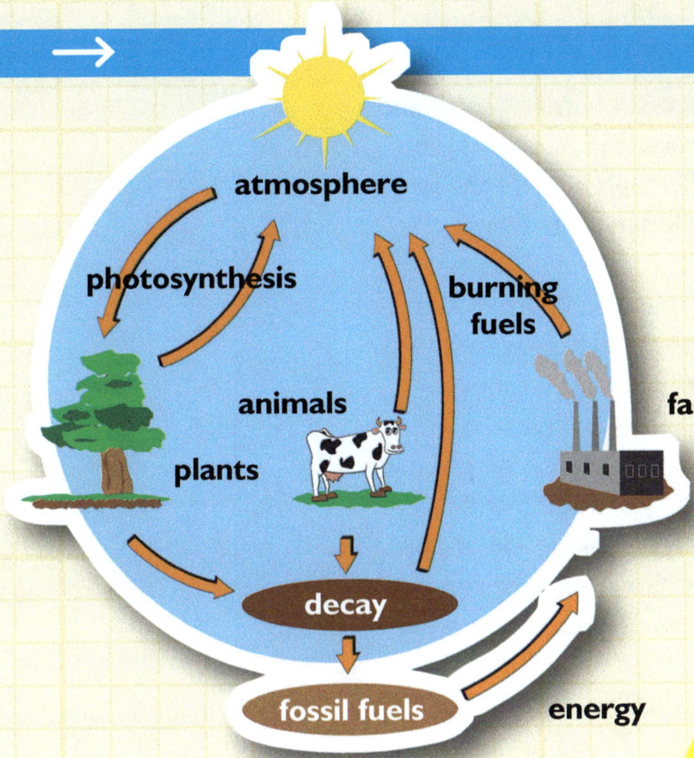

Animals feed on the plants, passing the carbon along the food chain.

Animals breathe out most of the carbon they consume. When animals and plants die and decompose, any carbon in their bodies returns to the atmosphere as carbon dioxide.

Flowchart Smart

Preventing Pollution

Pollution has many negative impacts on human health and the environment, but it can be prevented. Governments, businesses, communities, and individuals around the world can all play a part in beating pollution in all its forms.

Governments and leaders can increase or improve the laws preventing pollution and take stronger action against those who disobey those laws. Governments and businesses can clean up contaminated sites. They can invest in more renewable forms of energy and make it easier for people to choose a renewable energy supply. Another option is to impose **taxes**, for example on types of fuel or on the vehicles that cause most pollution. Governments can also raise people's awareness of pollution issues.

Individuals do not have to wait for leaders to act. We can reduce the amount of plastic we use. Take reusable bags to the store instead of using disposable plastic bags. Buy food from stores that use less plastic packaging. Eat more organic food, which is grown without the use of pesticides and fertilizers. Buy locally grown fruit or vegetables to reduce the fuel used to transport food long distances to stores. Reuse or recycle clothes and other products instead of throwing them in the trash. Turn off lights to reduce energy use. There are many things we can do to make pollution a thing of the past!

Reduce the impact of pollution by clearing trash from wild and natural places.

Recycling household waste reduces the amount of waste that is burned or sent to landfills.

Get Smart!

Unless people around the world take immediate action, the world's oceans will contain more plastic than fish by 2050.

Glossary

algae Plant-like living things that grow in damp places.

atmosphere The blanket of gases that surrounds Earth.

bacteria Tiny living things that can cause disease.

carbon dioxide A greenhouse gas formed when carbon is burned.

climate change A long-term change in Earth's weather patterns.

combustion Burning.

contaminate To make something dirty, polluted, or poisonous.

dissolves Breaks down and seems to disappear into a liquid such as water.

ecosystem A community of living things and the place where they live.

energy The capacity to do work.

environment The natural world.

fertilizers Chemicals farmers put on soil to help plants grow.

food chain A sequence of living things that depend on eating one another for survival.

fossil fuels Coal, oil, and natural gas formed from the remains of living things that died millions of years ago.

global warming An increase in temperatures around the world, caused by the greenhouse effect.

greenhouse gas Gas that traps heat in Earth's atmosphere.

groundwater Water that has collected deep underground.

microorganisms Living things so small they can only be seen under a microscope.

minerals Solid substances found naturally on Earth that make up rocks.

nutrients Substances that help living things grow.

organic To do with living things or things that were once alive.

organisms Living things.

particles Tiny fragments of a substance.

pesticides Chemicals that kill insects or other animals that damage crops.

photosynthesis The process by which plants produce their own food using carbon dioxide, water, and sunlight.

pollutants Substances that cause pollution.

sanitation systems Systems that safely remove human waste, such as urine and feces, from where people live.

taxes Amounts of money that people have to pay to the government.

toxic Poisonous.

water vapor The gas form of water.

For More Information

Books

Braun, Eric. *Taking Action to Help the Environment*. Minneapolis, MN: Lerner Publications, 2017.

Green, Jen. *50 Things You Should Know About the Environment*. Lake Forest, CA: QEB Publishing, 2016.

Jones, Keisha. *Halting Pollution*. New York, NY: PowerKids Press, 2017.

Smith-Llera, Danielle. *Trash Vortex: How Plastic Pollution Is Choking the World's Oceans*. North Mankato, MN: Compass Point Books, 2018.

Websites

Read more about pollution at:
eschooltoday.com/pollution/air-pollution/what-is-air-pollution.html

Visit this site for information about different types of water pollution:
www.explainthatstuff.com/waterpollution.html

Discover more about air pollution and global warming at:
www.nationalgeographic.com/environment/global-warming/pollution

Learn more about the problems pollution causes at:
www.worldwildlife.org/threats/pollution

Publisher's note to educators and parents: Our editors have carefully reviewed these websites to ensure that they are suitable for students. Many websites change frequently, however, and we cannot guarantee that a site's future contents will continue to meet our high standards of quality and educational value. Be advised that students should be closely supervised whenever they access the Internet.

Index